NFL TEAM STORIES

The Story of the

PHILADELPHIA EAGLES

By Jim Gigliotti

Kaleidoscope
Minneapolis, MN

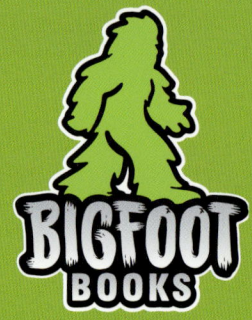

The Quest for Discovery Never Ends

....

This edition first published in 2021 by Kaleidoscope Publishing, Inc.

No part of this publication may be reproduced in whole or in part without written permission of the publisher.

For information regarding permission, write to Kaleidoscope Publishing, Inc.
6012 Blue Circle Drive
Minnetonka, MN 55343

Library of Congress Control Number
2020936025

ISBN
978-1-64519-243-5 (library bound)
978-1-64519-311-1 (ebook)

Text copyright © 2021 by Kaleidoscope Publishing, Inc. All-Star Sports, Bigfoot Books, and associated logos are trademarks and/or registered trademarks of Kaleidoscope Publishing, Inc.

Printed in the United States of America.

TABLE OF CONTENTS

Kickoff! 4

Chapter 1: Eagles History 6

Chapter 2: Eagles All-Time Greats 16

Chapter 3: Eagles Superstars 22

Beyond the Book 28
Research Ninja 29
Further Resources 30
Glossary 31
Index 32
Photo Credits 32
About the Author 32

KICKOFF!

The city of Philadelphia celebrated. People cheered. Car horns **blared**. Strangers hugged one another. The Eagles had won the Super Bowl! It was the 2017 season. The Eagles beat the mighty New England Patriots. Eagles fans waited a long time for that day. It was their first NFL title in 57 years. They have often had a lot to cheer about, though. This franchise started way back in the 1930s. Let's learn more about the Eagles.

FUN FACT
Philly police said that more than 700,000 people came to watch the Eagles parade.

Chapter 1
Eagles History

The Eagles began play in 1933. There were only nine other NFL teams at the time. This was a period called the Great Depression. It was a tough time for America. Many people were out of work. The government helped with a program called the New Deal. The logo for the New Deal had an eagle. That is how the Eagles got their name.

The National Recovery Act was part of the New Deal. The Eagles' owners were inspired by this NRA logo!

The Eagles Bill Hewitt makes a catch in 1939. Yes, he played without a helmet!

The Eagles were the NFL's best team in the late 1940s. They reached the title game in 1947. They lost that year. They won the title the next two years. They won both games by **shutout**. That is an NFL record. Running back Steve Van Buren was the big star. He scored the only touchdown in the 1948 title game.

THE STEAGLES

The Eagles were part of a unique team in 1943. Many players were fighting in World War II. The Eagles combined with the Steelers to form one team. It officially was called "Phil-Pitt." It unofficially was called the "Steagles." The Steagles finished with a winning record.

The field was white with snow during the 1948 NFL title game.

The Eagles beat the Chicago Cardinals 7–0. That game is called the "Snow Bowl." Heavy snow made the field a blanket of white!

Chuck Bednarik (60) makes the stop!

The Eagles' next championship came in 1960. They beat the Packers in the title game. Hall of Famer Norm Van Brocklin was the quarterback. Chuck Bednarik played the entire game. He was a center on offense. He was a linebacker on defense. He made a tackle on the final play to save the win.

The Eagles had some pretty good teams after that. They just could not quite make it to the top. They came close. The Eagles won the NFC in 1980. They lost the Super Bowl to the Raiders. They won the NFC again in 2004. They lost the Super Bowl to the Patriots. The team made the playoffs 16 times from 1988–2013.

The Patriots wrapped up the Eagles in Super Bowl XXXIX.

Then came the 2017 season. The Eagles won 13 games. That tied a team record set in 2004. They won the NFC. This time they beat the Patriots in the Super Bowl. Eagles fans **rejoiced**!

The team has stayed near the top ever since. The Eagles made the playoffs again in 2018. They won their division in 2019. These are high-flying times for a proud team!

FUN FACT
The Super Bowl trophy is named for famed Packers coach Vince Lombardi.

Nick Foles with the Lombardi Trophy.

TIMELINE OF THE PHILADELPHIA EAGLES

1933
1933: The Eagles begin play.

1949
1949: The team wins its second title in a row.

1960
1960: The Eagles beat the Packers in the NFL title game.

1980
1980: The team wins its first NFC title.

2004
2004: The Eagles win 13 games and the NFC title.

2017
2017: The Eagles win the Super Bowl for the first time.

2019
2019: The team makes the playoffs for the third year in a row.

A PHILLY SURPRISE!

The Eagles beat the Patriots in the Super Bowl in the 2017 season. The big play of the game was a trick play. Here is what happened.

The Eagles were ahead 15–12. It was a very tight game. Philly needed more points.

They had the ball right before halftime. It was fourth down at the Patriots' 1-yard line. Should they kick an easy field goal? Or should they go for the touchdown? The Eagles decided to go for it.

Quarterback Nick Foles walked toward the line of scrimmage. He pretended to call signals. But the Eagles snapped the ball to running back Corey Clement. He flipped the ball to tight end Trey Burton. Then Burton passed to Foles. The QB caught the ball in the end zone. Touchdown! The Patriots were stunned. The Eagles led 22–12. They won 41–33.

FUN FACT
The Eagles' name for this trick play was the "Philly Special."

Chapter 2
Eagles All-Time Greats

Defensive end Reggie White and linebacker Chuck Bednarik are the best players in Eagles history. They were huge forces on defense. Bednarik was really tough. He was called "Concrete Charlie." He was a star for the 1960 NFL champs. White was called the "Minister of Defense." He played 121 games for the team from 1985–92. He had 124 **sacks**!

Brian Dawkins was another great defender. He was a hard-hitting safety. He was always around the ball. He **intercepted** 34 passes from 1996–2008. All three players are in the Hall of Fame.

Chuck Bednarik

Reggie White

The Eagles have had some great running backs. Wilbert Montgomery and Brian Westbrook led the NFL in yards from scrimmage in a season. That means rushing and receiving yards combined. Montgomery did it in 1979. Westbrook did it in 2007. Ricky Watters rushed for more than 1,000 yards three years in a row beginning in 1995. LeSean McCoy had four 1,000-yard seasons for the team in the 2010s.

Steve Van Buren might have been the best back of them all. He topped the NFL in rushing four times in the 1940s.

LeSean McCoy

Steve Van Buren

The team has had some star quarterbacks in its history, too. Tommy Thompson guided the Eagles' first championship teams. He was one of the NFL's great passers of the 1940s. Norm Van Brocklin led the 1960 champs. He is in the Hall of Fame.

Randall Cunningham and Donovan McNabb were double threats. They were terrific passers. They also gained yards with their feet.

FUN FACT
McNabb was named to six Pro Bowls. That is the NFL's all-star game.

Donovan McNabb

EAGLES RECORDS

These players piled up the best stats in Eagles history. The numbers are career records through the 2019 season.

Total TDs: Harold Carmichael, 79

TD Passes: Donovan McNabb, 216

Passing Yards: Donovan McNabb, 32,873

Receiving Yards: Harold Carmichael, 8,978

Rushing Yards: LeSean McCoy, 6,792

Receptions: Harold Carmichael, 589

Points: David Akers, 1,323

Sacks: Reggie White, 124

Chapter 3
Eagles Superstars

The Eagles believe they have a big star in Carson Wentz. He is a strong-armed quarterback. The team drafted him in the first round in 2016. He passed for 33 touchdowns in only 13 games the next year. He took the team to the 2017 playoffs. He couldn't play in the Super Bowl, though. He was injured. He missed the 2018 playoffs, too. He was back for 2019. The team hopes he gets many more chances in the playoffs.

Carson Wentz looks for an open receiver.

Many of Carson Wentz's passes go to tight ends. Zach Ertz made the Pro Bowl for the third year in a row in 2019. Second-year man Dallas Goedert is right behind him. Goedert is becoming a star.

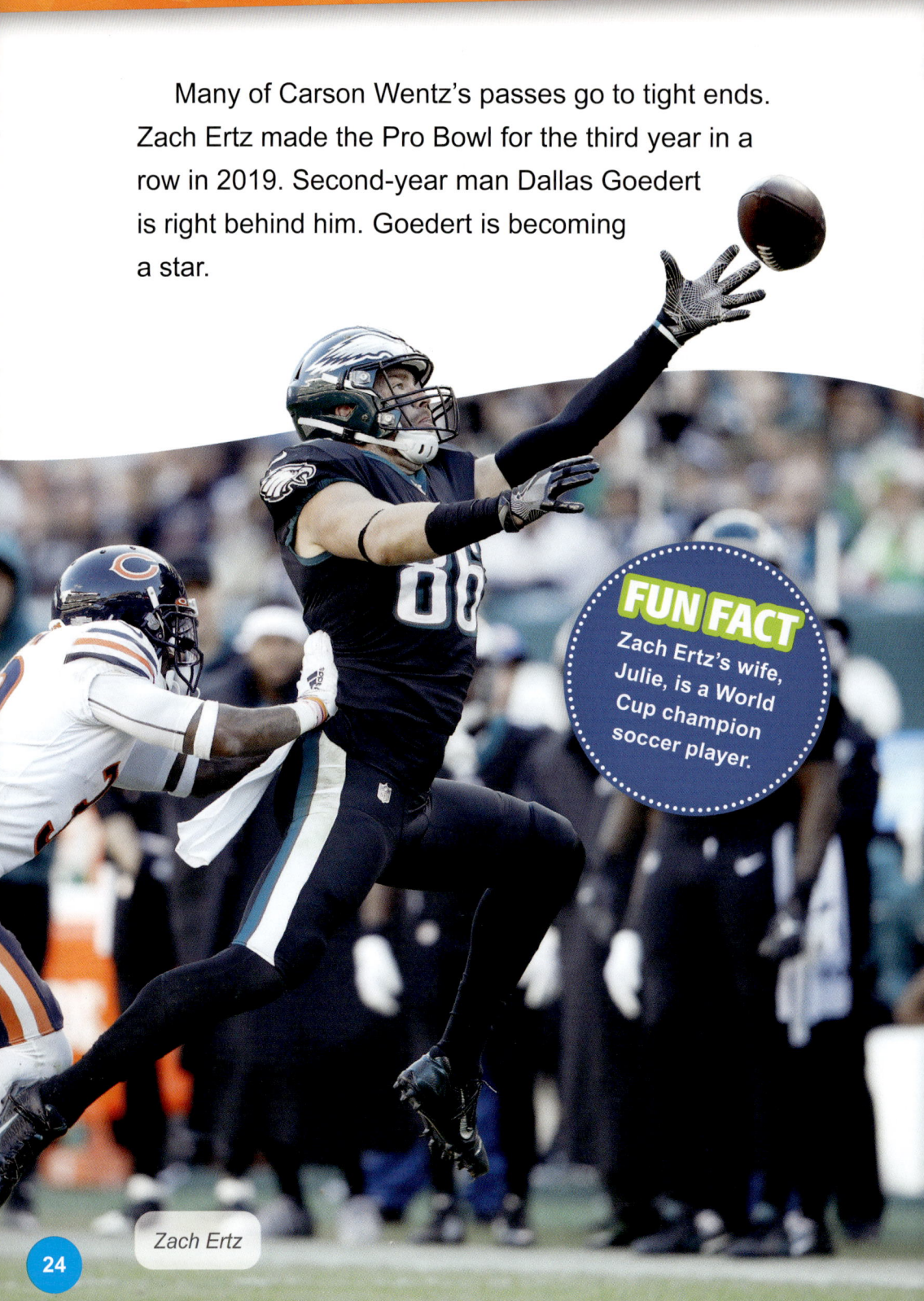

FUN FACT
Zach Ertz's wife, Julie, is a World Cup champion soccer player.

Zach Ertz

Miles Sanders

The Eagles also added a young running back in 2019. He is named Miles Sanders. He played behind New York Giants superstar Saquon Barkley in college. Sanders got his chance to shine for Penn State his final year. Then the Eagles drafted him. They were not disappointed! He was the team's leading rusher. He also caught 50 passes.

Fletcher Cox

The Eagles are really good on the defensive line. Fletcher Cox is a top defensive tackle. He is one of the best at getting to the quarterback. He made the Pro Bowl in 2019. It was his fifth all-star nod in a row.

Brandon Graham racks up sacks at defensive end. He led the Eagles with 8.5 sacks in 2019. Graham had one of his best games in the team's Super Bowl win in 2017. He sacked quarterback Tom Brady late in the game. It forced a fumble. It helped seal the Eagles' win.

With a great past, the Eagles hope to fly into a great future!

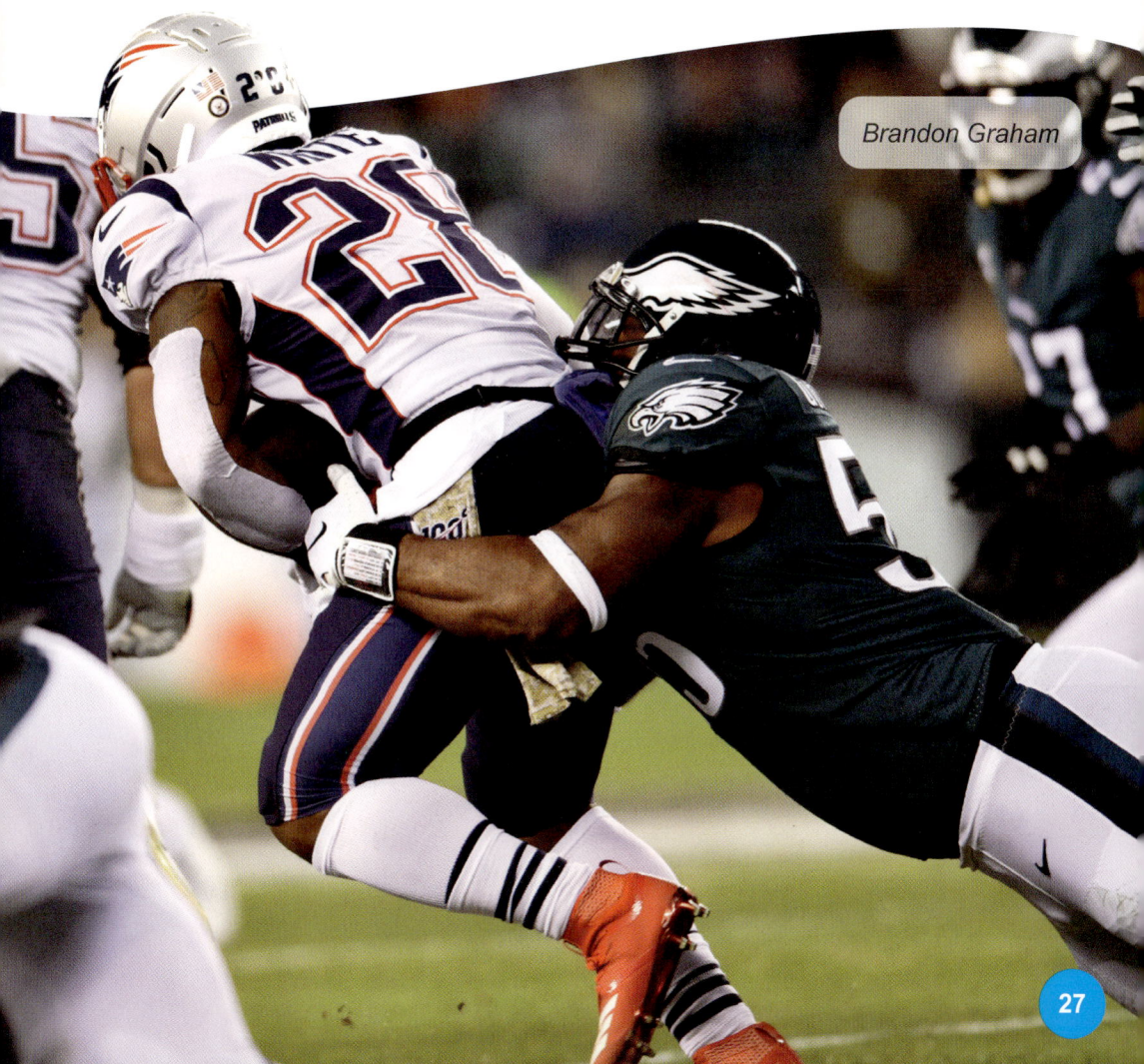

Brandon Graham

BEYOND
THE BOOK

After reading the book, it's time to think about what you learned. Try the following exercises to jumpstart your ideas.

RESEARCH

FIND OUT MORE. Where would you go to find out more about your favorite NFL teams and players? Check out NFL.com, of course. Each team also has its own website. What other sports information sites can you find? See if you can find other cool facts about your favorite team.

CREATE

GET ARTISTIC. Each NFL team has a logo. The Eagles logo shows a pair of eagle wings. Get some art materials and try designing your own Eagles logo. Or create a new team and make a logo for it. What colors would you choose? How would you draw the mascot?

DISCOVER

GO DEEP! In this book, you learned about the Phil-Pitt Steagles from 1943. Use your imagination and come up with some other "combo" NFL teams. What two (or more teams) would you put together? What odd nicknames would result?

GROW

GET OUT AND PLAY! You don't need to be in the NFL to enjoy football. You just need a football and some friends. Play touch or tag football. Or you can hang cloth flags from your belt; grab the belt and make the "tackle." See who has the best arm to be quarterback. Who is the best receiver? Who can run the fastest? Time to play football!

RESEARCH NINJA

Visit **www.ninjaresearcher.com/2435** to learn how to take your research skills and book report writing to the next level!

RESEARCH

DIGITAL LITERACY TOOLS

SEARCH LIKE A PRO
Learn about how to use search engines to find useful websites.

FACT OR FAKE?
Discover how you can tell a trusted website from an untrustworthy resource.

TEXT DETECTIVE
Explore how to zero in on the information you need most.

SHOW YOUR WORK
Research responsibly—learn how to cite sources.

WRITE

GET TO THE POINT
Learn how to express your main ideas.

PLAN OF ATTACK
Learn prewriting exercises and create an outline.

DOWNLOADABLE REPORT FORMS

Further Resources

BOOKS

Cooper, Robert. *Philadelphia Eagles (Inside the NFL)*. Mendota Heights, Minn: North Star Editions, 2019.

Editors of Sports Illustrated Kids. *1st and 10 (Revised and Updated): Top 10 Lists of Everything in Football*. New York: Sports Illustrated Kids, 2016.

Jacobs, Greg. *The Everything Kids' Football Book (Sixth Edition)*. Avon, Mass.: Adams Media, 2018.

WEBSITES

Factsurfer.com gives you a safe, fun way to find more information.

1. Go to www.factsurfer.com.
2. Enter "Philadelphia Eagles" into the search box and click 🔍
3. Select your book cover to see a list of related websites.

Glossary

blared: made a loud, sudden noise. The loudspeaker blared out the Eagles' fight song.

intercepted: when a defender catches a pass aimed at the offense. Dawkins stepped in front of the receiver and intercepted the ball.

Pro Bowl: the NFL's annual all-star game. The great Harold Carmichael was honored with four Pro Bowl selections.

rejoiced: cheered with joy. Eagles fans rejoiced when their team won the Super Bowl.

sacks: tackles of the quarterback behind the line of scrimmage. Michael Strahan was one of the NFL's best sack masters.

shutout: a game in which one team does not allow the other team to score any points. The Eagles beat the Patriots in a shutout, 34–0.

winning record: when a team wins more games than it loses. At 9–7 in 2019, the Eagles had a winning record.

World War II: a long battle among many nations that lasted from 1939–1945. America fought in World War II against Germany, Japan, and other nations.

Index

Bednarik, Chuck, 10, 16
Burton, Trey, 14
Chicago Cardinals, 9
Clement, Corey, 14
Cox, Fletcher, 26
Cunningham, Randall, 20
Dawkins, Brian, 16
Ertz, Zach, 24
Foles, Nick, 14
Goedert, Dallas, 24
Graham, Brandon, 27
Great Depression, 6
McCoy, LeSean, 18
McNabb, Donovan, 20

Montgomery, Wilbert, 18
National Recovery Act, 6
New England Patriots, 4, 11, 12, 14
Oakland Raiders, 11
Sanders, Miles, 25
Super Bowl, 4, 11, 12, 14, 22, 27
Thompson, Tommy, 20
Van Brocklin, Norm, 10, 20
Van Buren, Steve, 8, 18
Watters, Ricky, 18
Wentz, Carson, 22, 24
Westbrook, Brian, 18
White, Reggie, 16

PHOTO CREDITS

The images in this book are reproduced through the courtesy of: AP Images: Tony Tomsic 6; 14, 18; David Durochik 17. Focus on Football: 8, 9, 12, 16, 19, 20, 22, 25, 26. Newscom: Terry Gilliam/MCT 10; Zach Bollinger/Icon SW 11, 24, 27. **Cover photo:** Focus on Football.

About the Author

Jim Gigliotti was an editor at NFL Publishing for many years. Now he writes books for young readers.